D1288972

GLOBAL GHOST STORIES

GHOSTS IN AFRICA

BY CHRISTINA LEAF

EPIC

BELLWETHER MEDIA • MINNEAPOLIS, MN

EPIC BOOKS are no ordinary books. They burst with intense action, high-speed heroics, and shadows of the unknown. Are you ready for an Epic adventure?

This edition first published in 2022 by Bellwether Media, Inc.

Library of Congress Cataloging-in-Publication Data

Names: Leaf, Christina, author.
Title: Ghosts in Africa / by Christina Leaf.
Other titles: Epic. Global ghost stories.
Description: Minneapolis, MN : Bellwether Media, 2022. | Series: Epic: global ghost stories | Includes bibliographical references and index. | Audience: Ages 7-12 | Audience: Grades 4-6 | Summary: "Engaging images accompany information about ghost stories in Africa. The combination of high-interest subject matter and light text is intended for students in grades 2 through 7"--Provided by publisher.
Identifiers: LCCN 2021011393 (print) | LCCN 2021011394 (ebook) | ISBN 9781644875360 (library binding) | ISBN 9781648344442 (ebook)
Subjects: LCSH: Ghosts--Africa--Juvenile literature. | Haunted places--Africa--Juvenile literature.
Classification: LCC BF1472.A35 L43 2022 (print) | LCC BF1472.A35 (ebook) | DDC 133.1096--dc23
LC record available at https://lccn.loc.gov/2021011393
LC ebook record available at https://lccn.loc.gov/2021011394

Editor: Betsy Rathburn Designer: Brittany McIntosh

Printed in the United States of America, North Mankato, MN.

TABLE OF CONTENTS

GHOSTS IN AFRICA

Africa's many countries hold thousands of **cultures**. Among them float strange stories.

Some tell of wandering spirits. Others speak of **cursed** souls. Are the stories true? Could Africa be home to ghosts?

THE TREE SPIRIT

In West Africa grows the tall Iroko tree. The Yoruba people tell about the spirit of a man who lives in the tree.

The spirit wanders the forest at night, scaring travelers.

Iroko tree

The Yoruba believe it is bad luck to see the Iroko-man. Death comes quickly to those who do.

Cutting down the Iroko tree curses the cutter and their family. However, saying a prayer afterward can protect them.

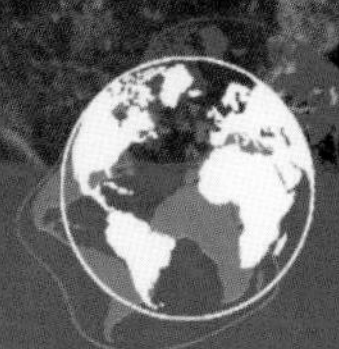

CULTURAL CONNECTION

A haunted baobab tree stands in Zambia. A ghostly python lives inside. Locals worshipped the snake until a white hunter killed it. But people still hear hissing in the tree!

Those who use iroko wood may be in danger, too.

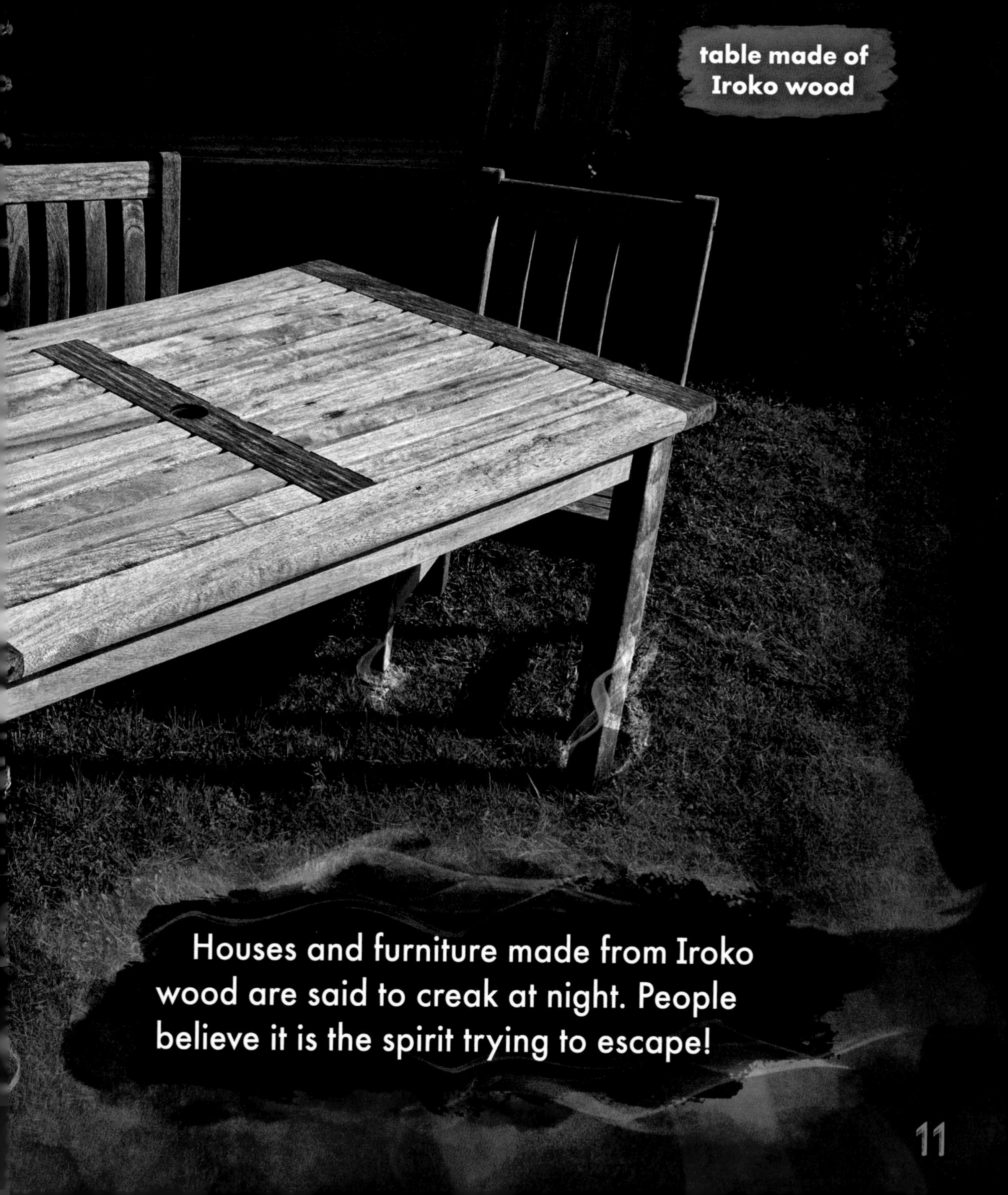

table made of Iroko wood

Houses and furniture made from Iroko wood are said to creak at night. People believe it is the spirit trying to escape!

THE VALLEY OF THE DEAD

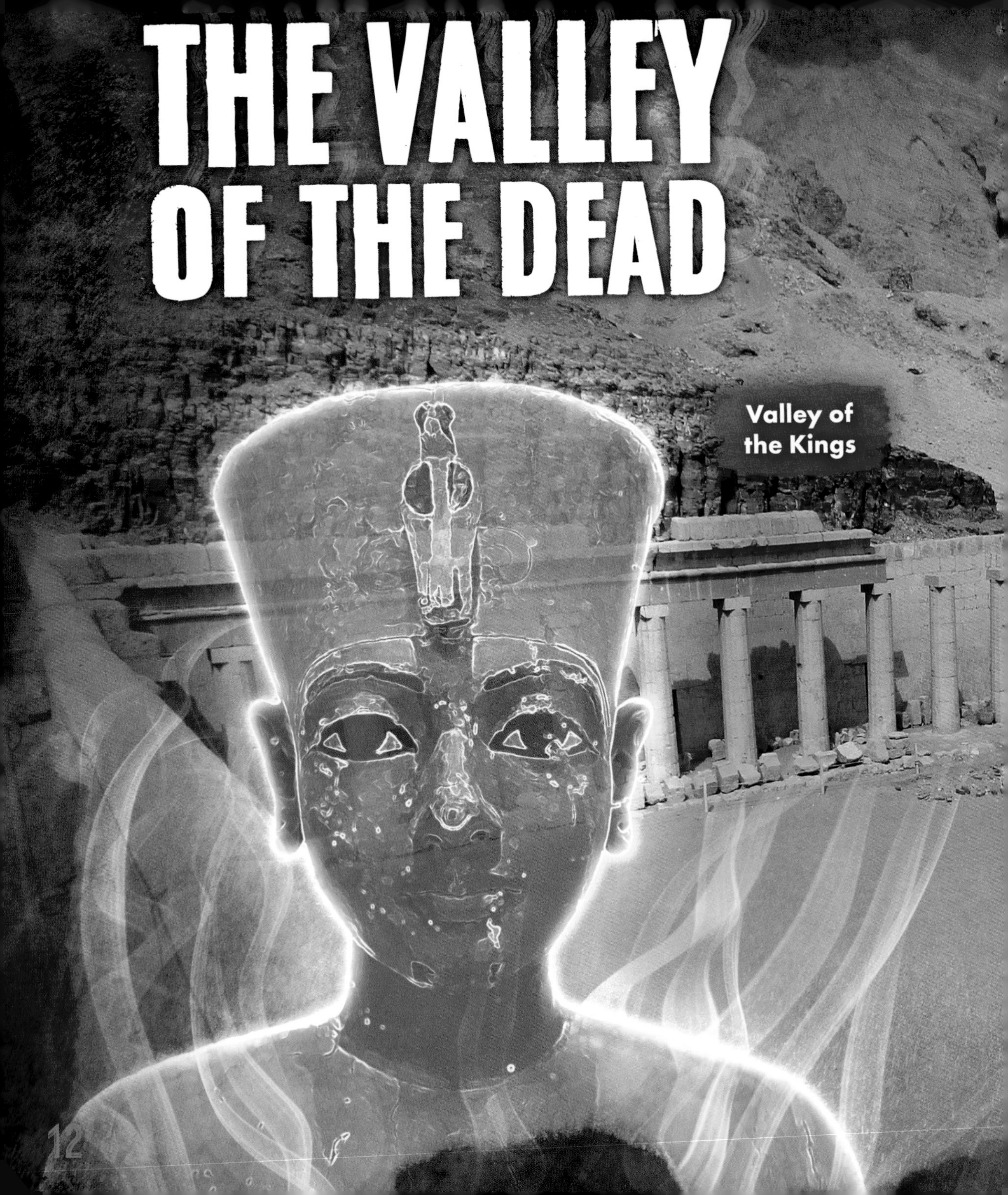

In Egypt's desert hides a grand burial place. The Valley of the Kings lies near Luxor.

Many of Egypt's **pharaohs** were laid to rest here. But are they really resting?

Night watchmen guard the **tombs**. They hear strange noises. Footsteps fall when no one is around. Screams and shouts break the desert's quiet.

People have even seen a ghostly **chariot** pulled by black horses!

Some believers think the noises are pharaohs. They are angry because their tombs were **disturbed**. Others believe the tombs are cursed.

THE GHOSTLY DESERT

Egypt may be full of ghosts! People believe a pharaoh's ghost haunts the Farafra Desert. He was said to be cursed by priests.

Either way, the tombs and mummies inside scare many visitors!

THE HAUNTED CRATER

Menengai Crater
Kenya

The Menengai **Crater** stands tall in Kenya. Long ago, a battle raged near this **volcano**. Two groups of Maasai people fought over land.

Eventually, the Ilpurko defeated the Ilaikipiak. The losing **warriors** were thrown into the volcano.

GODS OR DEVILS?

Menengai **means "place of many gods." But locals also call it *Kirima kia Ngoma*. This means "place of devils."**

People believe the warriors' spirits haunt the volcano. Visitors to the area have gotten lost. Some were found hours later, confused. Others have disappeared completely!

IS IT TRUE?

Some people do not believe the crater is haunted. Dangerous plants grow nearby. These can cause confusion and make people feel scared.

Is it the work of angry spirits?
What do you think?

GLOSSARY

chariot—a two-wheeled cart drawn by horses often used in battles or other events

crater—the bowl-shaped opening of a volcano

cultures—beliefs, arts, and ways of life in places or societies

cursed—under a harmful spell

disturbed—bothered

pharaohs—rulers in ancient Egypt

tombs—chambers where dead bodies are placed for burial

volcano—a hole in the earth; volcanoes shoot out hot ash, gas, or melted rock called lava when they erupt.

warriors—people who fight in battles and wars

TO LEARN MORE

AT THE LIBRARY

Bullis, Amber. *Famous Ghost Stories of Africa*. North Mankato, Minn.: Capstone Press, 2019.

Hoena, Blake. *The Mummy's Curse: Discovering King Tut's Tomb*. Minneapolis, Minn.: Bellwether Media, 2020.

Peterson, Megan Cooley. *The Flying Dutchman: The Doomed Ghost Ship*. North Mankato, Minn.: Capstone Press, 2020.

ON THE WEB

FACTSURFER

Factsurfer.com gives you a safe, fun way to find more information.

1. Go to www.factsurfer.com.

2. Enter "ghosts in Africa" into the search box and click 🔍.

3. Select your book cover to see a list of related content.

INDEX

The images in this book are reproduced through the courtesy of: Juliya Shangarey, front cover (top); Volodymyr Burdiak, front cover (bottom), pp. 2-3; Nick Fox, pp. 3; Chantal de Bruijne, pp. 4-5; AFRICAPEOPLEIMAGES, p. 5; Wolfgang Kaehler/ Alamy, pp. 6-7; Jorge Fernandez/ Alamy, p. 8; Xavier Desmier/ Getty Images, pp. 8-9; Ingrid Heres, p. 9; Michael Foley/ Alamy, pp. 10-11; Victor Jiang, p. 12; Zbigniew Guzowski, pp. 12-13, 14-15; Orhan Cam, p. 14; Rachelle Burnside, p. 16; Sergey-73, pp. 16-17; Ihor Voronin, p. 17 (pharaoh); pathdoc, p. 17 (woman); Dorling Kindersley ltd/ Alamy, pp. 18-19; Katiekk, pp. 19, 21 (top); GaudiLab, p. 20 (bottom); Martin Mwaura/ Alamy, p. 20 (bottom); Sopotnicki, p. 21 (bottom); Avatar_023, p. 22.